Adrenalin Rush

Alex Lane

Contents

OXFORD
UNIVERSITY PRESS

What do we mean by *extreme*?

Why go climbing when you can go *ice climbing*? Why go running when you can go *free running*? Some people love the feeling they get from doing dangerous sports. Dangerous sports are often called 'extreme' sports. They require a lot of skill in order to do them safely.

Warning!

All the sports mentioned in this book are extremely dangerous.

- Never try these sports at home.
- Never try these sports without proper supervision, proper training or proper equipment.

Why do people enjoy extreme sports?

Extreme sports push people mentally as well as physically. They can be scary, but they can also be very exciting. When you are scared or excited, your body produces *adrenalin*. Adrenalin is a chemical. It can help your body to react quicker and cope with stressful situations. It can therefore help improve a person's performance when doing an extreme sport. Some effects of adrenalin are:

Ice climbing

Imagine being freezing cold and stuck to the side of an ice-covered cliff for hours on end as you try to climb to the top!

Ice climbing is like rock climbing, but climbers climb frozen ice formations – glaciers, frozen waterfalls and rock faces that are covered with snow and ice. Ice climbing is more dangerous than rock climbing. This is because ice constantly changes according to weather conditions. Ice is less **predictable** than rock.

This climber is scaling a frozen waterfall.

Equipment

Clothing: warm clothing is essential as climbers are out in freezing conditions for long periods of time.

Helmet: a helmet will help protect a climber's head if they fall or if something falls on them!

Gloves: climbers wear gloves or mittens to keep their hands warm. They don't grip the surface of the ice directly with their hands the way rock climbers do.

Boots and crampons: ice climbers need a good, strong pair of climbing boots which give support round the ankles. Crampons are metal spikes attached to the bottom of boots. These help the climber to grip to the ice. The forward spikes can be kicked into the ice to gain footholds.

Ice axe: an axe is used to grip the ice. Axes are made from metal and normally have a **serrated** edge. A cord on the handle is wrapped around the climber's wrist to ensure that the axe is not dropped by accident.

Harness: this is used to attach a climber to their rope. It helps them climb up and **abseil** down.

Rope: a rope is an essential piece of safety equipment. It is used to stop climbers falling all the way to the ground.

Ice screws: these are screwed into the ice. Rope can be threaded through them for safety. Ice screws are strong and can hold a lot of weight.

Safety and hazards

You need to be very fit to be able to ice climb, but good technique is just as important as being strong. Before a climber can start on ice, they must develop good overall climbing skills. These include: basic climbing **manoeuvres**, **belaying**, rope tying, lowering and abseiling, and safety and hazard evaluation.

Climbing hazards

Ice climbers face many hazards, such as:

- soft and melting ice
- avalanches and falling ice
- changing weather conditions
- falling rocks
- extreme cold
- sharp tools that climbers carry.

These two ice climbers are climbing the Korouoma Canyon in Posio, Finland.

Fact box: Avalanches

An avalanche is a mass of ice and snow that breaks away from a mountainside. It travels at great speed. Avalanches can happen quickly and are very dangerous. They are caused when the slope underneath the snow becomes unstable and can no longer support the weight of snow and ice on top. They can be caused by snowstorms, heavy snowfalls, explosions and earth tremors.

Freediving

German diver, Tom Sietas broke the record for holding his breath underwater in 2008. He managed to hold his breath for an incredible 10 minutes and 12 seconds.

Freediving is a sport where divers **descend** underwater on a single breath of air. They do not use any breathing equipment. Every year, freediving competitions are held all around the world.

Events and records

STATIC APNEA

Description: Freedivers stay underwater for as long as possible. It is always done under proper supervision.

Male record holder:
Name: Tom Sietas (Germany)
Result: 10 mins 12 secs
Date: 7th June 2008

Female record holder:
Name: Natalia Molchanova (Russia)
Result: 8 mins
Date: 6th July 2008

CONSTANT WEIGHT

Description: Freedivers dive down as far as possible. They follow a guide line which measures the depth of the dive. They are not allowed to touch the line.

Male record holder:
Name: Guillaume Néry (France)
Result: 86 metres (m)
Date: 3rd July 2008

Female record holder:
Name: Natalia Molchanova (Russia)
Result: 95 m
Date: 25th July 2008

DYNAMIC APNEA

Description: Freedivers travel through the water horizontally as far as possible.

Male record holder:
Name: Alexey Molchanov (Russia)
Result: 250 m
Date: 5th October 2008

Female record holder:
Name: Natalia Molchanova (Russia)
Result: 214 m
Date: 5th October 2008

FREE IMMERSION

Description: Freedivers use a guide line to pull themselves down as far as possible and back up again. No fins are used.

Male record holder:
Name: William Trubridge (New Zealand)
Result: 108 m
Date: 11th April 2008

Female record holder:
Name: Natalia Molchanova (Russia)
Result: 85 m
Date: 27th July 2008

VARIABLE WEIGHT

Description: Freedivers descend with the help of weights. They return to the surface by pulling themselves up along a line or by swimming.

Male record holder:
Name: Carlos Costa (Venezuela)
Result: 140 m
Date: 9th May 2008

Female record holder:
Name: Tanya Streeter (USA)
Result: 122 m
Date: 19th July 2008

NO LIMIT

Description: Freedivers can use any means to dive down as far as possible and return to the surface as long as a guide line is used to measure the distance.

Male record holder:
Name: Herbert Nitsch (Austria)
Result: 214 m
Date: 14th June 2008

Female record holder:
Name: Tanya Streeter (USA)
Result: 160 m
Date: 17th August 2008

Equipment

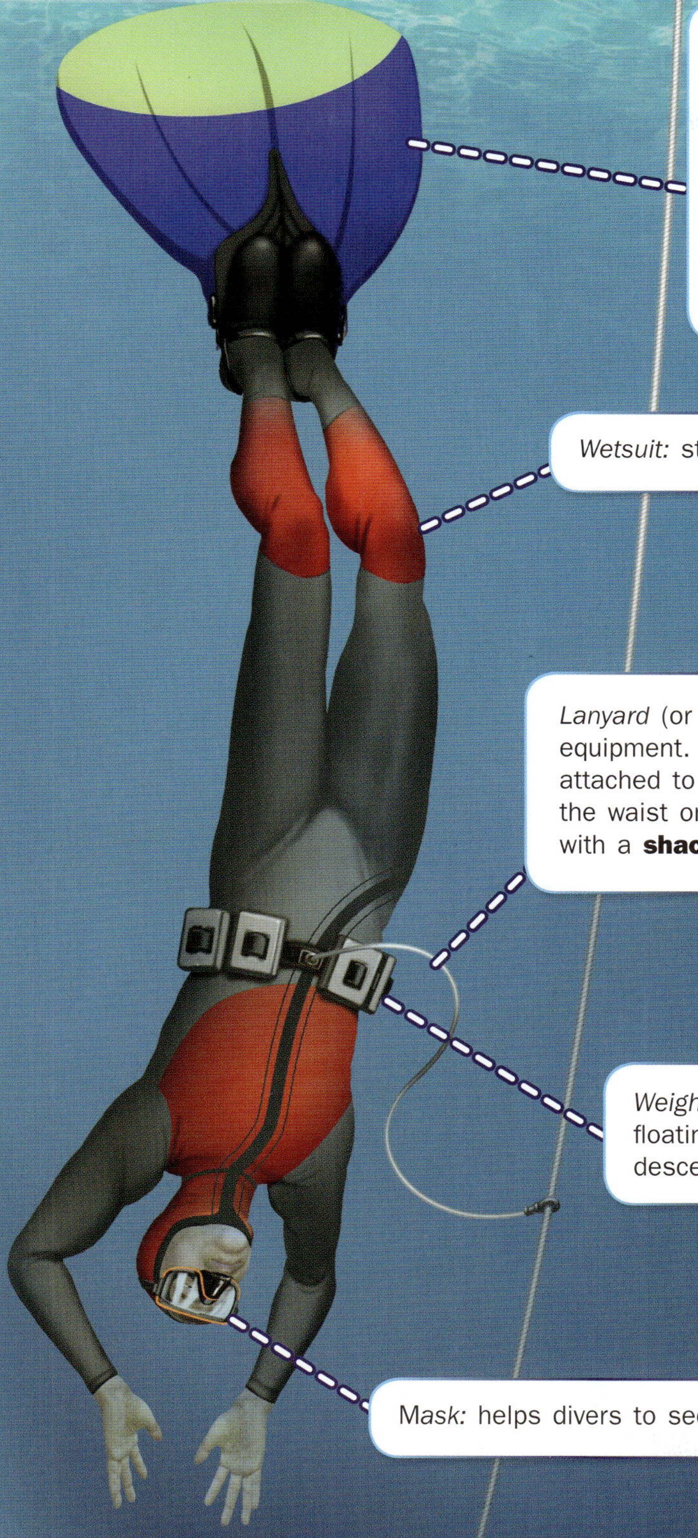

Fins: help divers move easily through the water. They produce a wave of water that pushes the freediver forward. There are two types of fins: bi-fins (one fin on each foot) and mono-fins (one fin attached to both feet – think of the tail of a dolphin).

Wetsuit: stops divers from getting cold.

Lanyard (or *leash*): a piece of safety equipment. It is a length of cord that is attached to the freediver at one end (at the waist or wrist); the other end is fitted with a **shackle** to the guide line.

Weights: helps to stop divers floating and allows them to descend more easily.

Mask: helps divers to see underwater.

What happens to your body?

The deeper a freediver goes, the greater the water pressure is around them. This has several effects on the body.

- The pressure on the ears increases. The eardrum is pushed inwards.
- The heart rate slows.
- Blood is drawn away from external parts of the body (hands, feet, etc) to the vital organs (heart, brain, etc).
- More oxygen is sent to the lungs.

Try this ...

<u>Water pressure experiment</u>

What you need:

1 x bucket or bowl filled with water

1 x empty plastic drinking bottle (with the lid on)

What you need to do:

Slowly submerge (sink) the bottle into your bucket or bowl of water. As you push down, water pressure increases around it and the pressure on the sides of the container is increased. Imagine that the bottle is your ribcage. This is like the pressure a freediver feels as they dive down.

Try this ...

Ask an adult to look up Guillaume Néry or William Trubridge on YouTube, and watch how these two freedivers do it!

BASE jumping

You may have heard of skydiving (jumping out of an aeroplane). But have you heard of BASE jumping? BASE jumping is the sport of parachuting from fixed objects. Objects, or *jumping platforms*, include: cliffs, roller-coasters, buildings, cranes and bridges – anything that is tall enough and vertical enough to jump from! Jumps can be made from as low as 30 metres, but almost anything vertical and over 60 metres can be used as a jumping platform. Jumpers **free-fall** for a set period of time before they open their parachutes.

Fact box: BASE

BASE is an acronym. It stands for:
B: Building (any tall building)
A: Antenna (pylons)
S: Span (bridges)
E: Earth (cliffs)

These are the things that athletes jump from.

BASE jumper Simon Brentford jumps off of a wind turbine at an organized event in Norfolk, UK.

Interview with Max Hurd – BASE jumper

Max Hurd started skydiving in 1992. He moved on to BASE jumping four years later. Max has completed over four hundred jumps around the world.

How popular is BASE jumping?

There are currently only about a thousand people across the world who BASE jump. In the UK there are about fifty people who do it regularly. There is a strong emphasis on safety. As equipment, knowledge and skills get better, it is gradually growing in popularity.

Why do you do it?

It is a very personal thing. To me, it is like an exploration. I do it because I want to expand my knowledge and I want to experience new things. I also get to use all my **analytical** skills.

Where did you train?

The route in to BASE jumping is through skydiving. You have to do a minimum of two hundred skydives in order to develop the necessary skills. Then you need training from other BASE jumpers. You need to know what to do when something goes wrong and how to deal with it safely. It needs to become instinctive.

This is Max jumping off a cliff in Eastbourne, UK.

What equipment do you need?

You have one main parachute. You also have a pilot chute which is a small round parachute which you can hold in your hand and throw into the air. This helps to **deploy** the main parachute. There is no reserve parachute like you have with skydiving.

What do you wear?

You usually wear your normal, comfortable clothes. Most people wear boots with ankle supports to help protect them when landing. People also wear helmets and knee pads.

Have you ever hurt yourself?

Just a badly bruised toe! I landed once, ran a couple of steps and kicked a rock. Safety is important. I have walked away from jumps before because they do not 'feel' right. I also always take someone with me in case there are any accidents.

These are some of Max's bigger jumps!

How do you prepare for a jump?
Each jump is very carefully planned. You have to do a lot of preparation. You cannot work it out as you go! You have to take into account lots of different variables such as: your jump height, and wind and weather conditions. You also have to think about how the parachute will work at a certain height and in a certain place. You need to know about how wind moves and swirls around an object. What could be perfect conditions for the object may not apply thirty minutes later.

What was your favourite jump?
I went to Mexico and jumped into a big hole in the ground. It is called Sótano de las Golondrinas (Cave of the Swallows). It's 304 metres deep. The landing area is tight and you are jumping into darkness. It is quite intimidating.

What was your scariest jump?
They are all scary. It's being able to control your fear that is part of the discipline. It's only dangerous if you are not prepared. There is no margin for error.

Max jumping off a cliff in Switzerland.

Kitesurfing

Have you ever flown a kite? Imagine doing it while standing on a board in the sea. Kitesurfing is one of the fastest growing extreme water sports in the world. Kitesurfers stand on boards and use the wind to power large kites across open water. They can perform jumps and tricks if they fly the kite in a certain way. They can also go very fast – up to 50 knots.

Fact box: Knots

The term 'knots' comes from an old sailing method for telling the speed of a ship. A log would be thrown into the water with a length of knotted rope tied to it. This was left to trail behind the ship. The number of knots in the rope that were passed into the water in a given time would determine the speed in 'knots'.

Speed in knots	Speed in nautical miles per hour	Speed in miles per hour	Speed in kilometres per hour
1	1	1.15	1.85
10	10	11.5	18.5
50	50	57.5	92.6

Equipment

Compared to other water sports, you don't need a lot of equipment to kitesurf. This is one of the reasons why it is becoming so popular. Equipment should be checked regularly for signs of wear and tear.

Kites: most kitesurfing kites have a series of inflatable tubes. These 'grab' the wind – much like the sail of a sailing ship. They are controlled with handles or bars. It is extremely important that a kitesurfer can fly and control their kite before they go out on the water.

Helmets: wearing helmets is strongly encouraged to prevent head injuries.

Harness: the person in control of the kite is called the *pilot*. The kite is fastened to the pilot's waist by a harness. The kite is not attached to the board.

Boards: kiteboards can come in a wide variety of shapes and sizes. They look like snowboards or surfboards.

Fact box: Kitesurfing hazards

Can you think why these hazards might be dangerous?

- Sudden changes in water conditions
- Strong tides
- Strong winds
- High waves
- Water temperature
- Equipment failure
- Human error
- Hidden dangers (e.g. rocks, sandbanks)
- Dangerous animals (e.g. jellyfish).

Riding styles

Freestyle
Kitesurfers show off their skills. They use the board and the kite to gain height and do big jumps, rotations and tricks.

Speed
Kitesurfers use strong winds to go as fast as possible.

Boardercross
Kitesurfers have to get round a course, marked out by buoys, and perform tricks. The winner is the pilot who crosses the finish line first. This is one of the most dangerous disciplines. It combines freestyle and speed.

Wave riding
Kitesurfers ride waves like a surfboarder.

Hangtime
Kitesurfers do huge jumps and stay in the air for as long as possible.

Kickers and sliders
Kitesurfers perform tricks using ramps and rails that are placed in the water.

Freeride
Anything goes! Freeride is all about having fun!

This kitesurfer is performing a freestyle move. A smooth landing is the key to a good move.

Free running

Free running is an **urban** sport. Athletes jump, somersault, vault, roll and run to get from one place to another. They use buildings, walls, steps, railings and other structures as they run, jump and perform stunts.

Free running developed from another sport called *parkour*. Parkour uses similar moves, but it is about getting from A to B in the most efficient way possible. Free running is not about speed. Athletes can take their time. Both parkour and free running take lots of training, **stamina** and courage to be able to do them properly.

Jonny Last takes a massive leap on to a wall, Reading, UK.

Interview with Jonny Last – free runner

Jonny Last is training to be an actor and stuntman. He has been free running for over 6 years.

How did you get interested in free running?

I struggled at school with reading because I am dyslexic. So I was looking for an outlet for my energy. When I was 14, I saw an advert on TV where a man was getting from work to his home. The man was David Belle and he was doing parkour. As soon as I saw it, I knew I had to have a go.

What type of training have you done?

When I first started I thought you could just jump off of things. I didn't realize the consequences then. If you do that you will just get hurt. Your body has to be in top condition to free run. You have to be strong and fit. I have always done martial arts – karate, judo, kung fu, tai chi, and now capoeira (see page 31). *I have done gymnastics and pilates for inner core strength. I also teach breakdancing. I stretch every morning and every night. The first thing to do is to make sure you warm up properly.*

Do you have people that you train with?

I have some really close friends who I train with. There are about six of us. We help each other. It's great because we all have completely different skills and strengths. It's really important to have people who you look up to as well – someone at a much higher standard who you aspire to be like.

Who are your role models?

David Belle – the founder of parkour in France
Daniel Ilabaca – a Liverpool-born free runner
Chase Armitage – an actor and free runner
Cyril Raffaelli – an acrobat who got into parkour.

Do you get scared?

Yes. Sometimes. I always assess the situation. If I'm really scared I don't do it. I always check out a route before I try it. You have to know your area. If you don't know your area you are going to hurt yourself. It's dangerous, for example, when it's wet and slippery. Having good technique is really important at times like this. You have to practise a lot before you attempt anything big. You have to start small. Learn techniques bit by bit.

Where do you practise free running?

I live in Oxford, so I practise all round the city. By free running, I can get to places other people can't. It's a great way to see a city! You get to really appreciate all the different buildings.

Why do you do it?

It is the most amazing feeling in the world. To get a new somersault that you have been practising for ages feels great. When I find something I like doing I stick to it and have to make myself the best I can be. It is about freedom.

What mental and physical skills do you need to be a free runner?

A positive mental attitude. A strong, fit body. Determination and confidence.

Try this ...

Sébastien Foucan is another parkour founder. Look him up on the Internet.

BMX

Motorcross is cross-country racing on motorbikes. BMX is a version of this using bicycles. BMX, therefore, stands for *Bicycle Motorcross*. As well as racing, people can also do stunts and tricks on BMX bikes. This is called *freestyle*.

BMX bikes are tough and light. The wheels are normally 51 or 61 centimetres in diameter. The wheels on a normal bike are 69 centimetres. Having smaller wheels on BMX bikes helps riders to **accelerate** fast and turn quickly.

BMX racing

BMX racing is fast and furious and very exciting to watch as well as take part in. Up to 8 riders race round a track 300–400 metres long. They go over jumps and banked corners called *berms*. The rider has to be skilled enough to negotiate the obstacles whilst going as fast as possible. Races consist of a number of qualifying races or *motos*. The rider who crosses the line first, wins.

Freestyle BMX

The term 'freestyle' covers all other types of BMX riding. It involves performing tricks over ramps or obstacles. There are five types of freestyle:

1) *Street*: riders perform tricks on and over obstacles in the street – on banks, walls, rails, gaps, etc.

2) *Park*: riders compete in specially designed skateparks, which have obstacles in them such as banks and mini ramps.

3) *Flatland*: riders perform tricks on flat ground. Tricks are performed by spinning and balancing in a variety of body and bicycle positions.

4) *Trails* (dirt jumping): riders carry out tricks over jumps built from dirt. Jumps have a steep take-off mound and a less steep landing mound.

5) *Vert*: this involves doing tricks on a special U-shaped ramp. The sides of the ramp are steep which makes it one of the most extreme and dangerous forms of BMX.

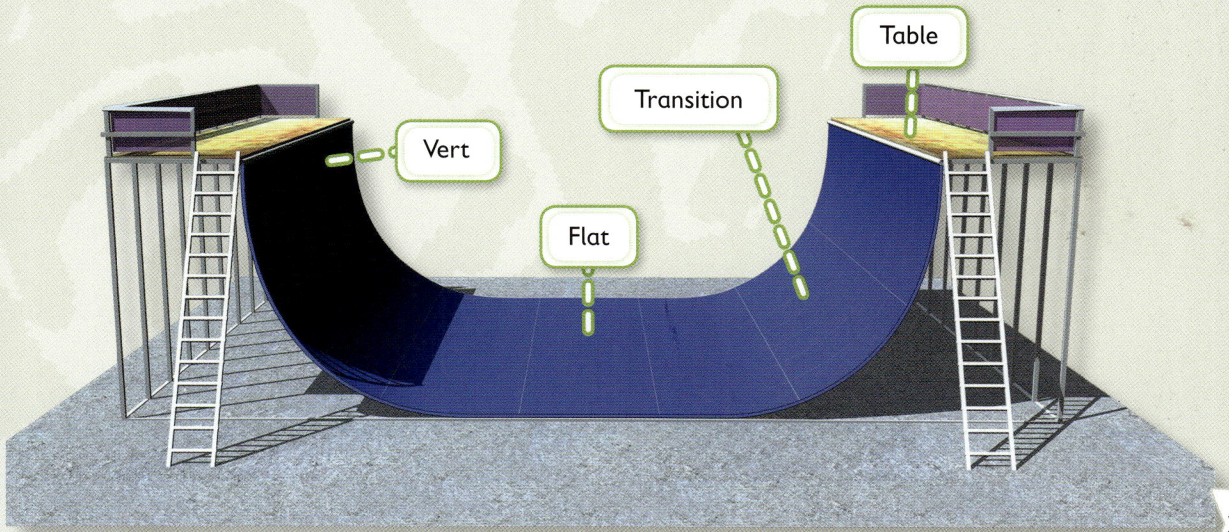

Hardcore sitting

Aaron Fotheringham

Aaron Fotheringham is a wheelchair athlete. He has invented a new type of extreme sport called *Hardcore sitting*. Aaron performs tricks and stunts in his wheelchair, similar to BMX riders and skateboarders. At the age of 14, he successfully performed the first ever backflip in a wheelchair.

Aaron was born on 8th November, 1991 in Las Vegas, USA. He has spina bifida which is a birth defect. It affects the spine and central nervous system. He has been a wheelchair user since the age of eight.

Aaron performs a stunt in a skatepark.

Interview with Aaron Fotheringham – Hardcore sitter

Did you come up with the name 'Hardcore sitting'?
Yes, Hardcore sitting (HCS) is a term that I thought up for extreme wheelchairing in skateparks.

How and when did you start Hardcore sitting?
My older brother, Brian, used to BMX and so he inspired me to start riding in skateparks. That was back in 2000.

How does it make you feel?
It makes me feel like I'm alive and not just playing video games.

What do you find hardest?
Coming up with new tricks is the hardest thing I've found. And then after you come up with the trick, then you actually have to land it!

How much time do you spend practising during each session?
It depends on the weather, but it can range from 2–8 hours.

What is your favourite trick?
The handplant. This is where you go up the quarter pipe [a curved, sloped ramp] *and stall* [balance] *on one hand (see picture above).*

How did you feel when you did your first record-breaking back flip?
I was speechless! It was amazing. After all my hard work, I got my reward.

Are there any tricks that you haven't been able to do yet?
It's not that I'm not able, it's just that I can't find a big enough ramp to be able to do them on!

Where would you like to see Hardcore sitting go in the future?
I want to see it as a category in X Games [X Games is an extreme sports competition that is held every year in summer and winter].

Caving

Caving is a great activity for those who don't mind small spaces, the dark, or spiders! Exploring a cave can be challenging and exciting – cavers go to places that no one has ever been before – but it is also important that they are properly prepared. Here are some essentials that every caver needs:

Caving hazards

Hypothermia: caves can be cold and wet. If a caver's body loses too much heat, then they get very ill. Wearing the right kind of clothing is essential.

Falls: unfortunately accidents do happen. This is why it is important never to go caving alone. Even experienced cavers should go caving with at least two other people. In an emergency, one person should stay with the injured person and the other can go for help.

Getting lost: it is possible to become **disorientated** in a cave, so it is important for cavers to look around often to get their bearings.

Getting stuck: caves often have tight spaces and it is possible to get stuck – although this does not happen often.

Falling objects: proper caves (as opposed to manmade tunnels – mines, etc) are generally very stable. However, there may be boulders, rocks or rubble that can come loose. A hard hat is essential.

Flooding: some caves can flood. It is important to get expert advice before going into a new cave.

Two cavers exploring *Rat's Nest Cave*, Alberta, Canada.

Ten top caves

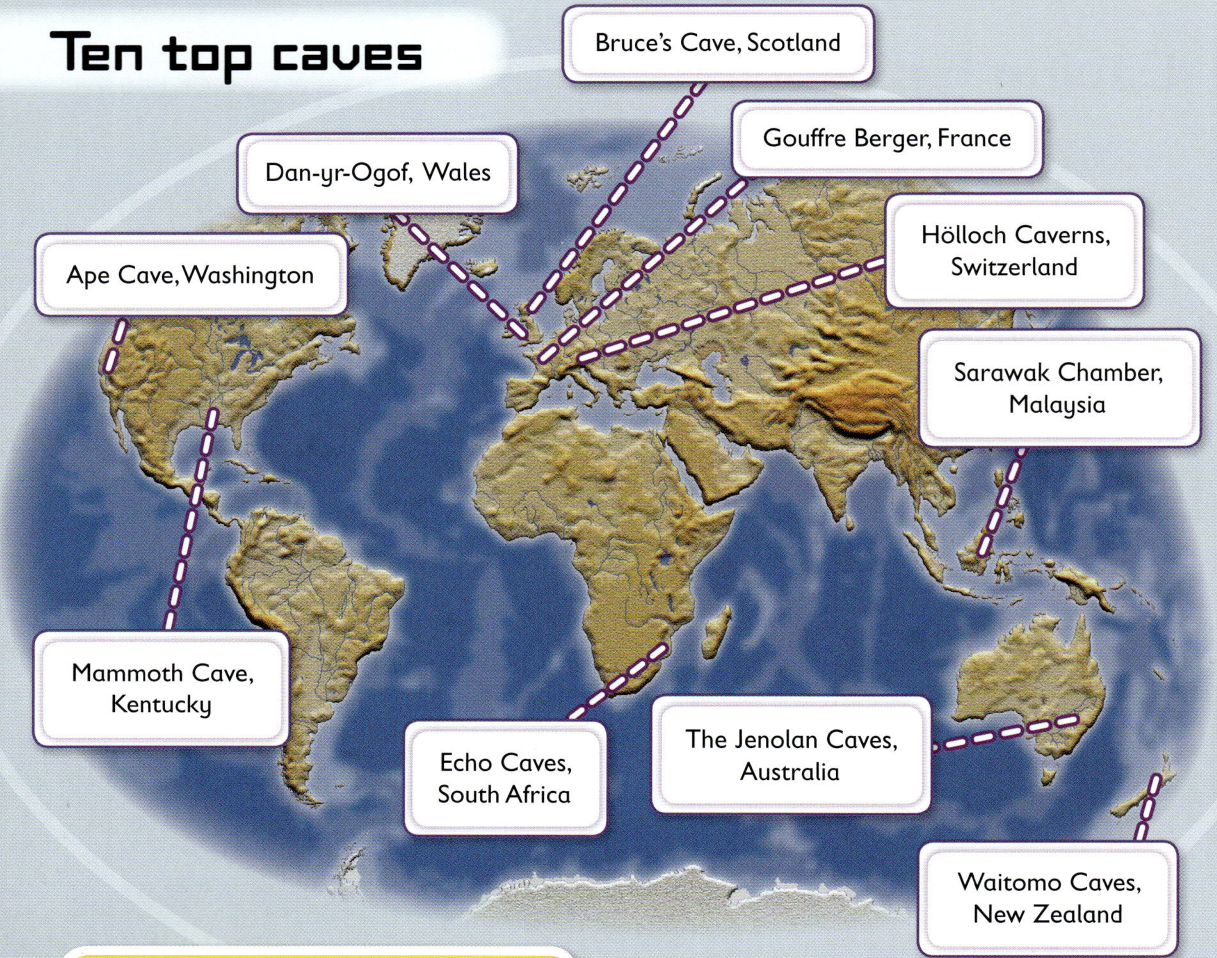

Fact box: Types of caves

- *Solution caves* are formed very slowly by water which dissolves the rock.
- *Talus caves* are formed between rocks that have fallen into piles.
- *Fracture caves* are formed between layers of rock.
- *Glacier caves* are found in ice and under glaciers.
- *Lava caves* are found near volcanoes which have been formed by flowing lava.
- *Sea caves* are found along coastlines and are mostly formed by the wave action of the sea.

A solution cave.

Martial arts

Martial arts are skills that you learn to help your body to become fit, supple and strong. They help teach you mental skills such as discipline, respect and self control. Someone trained in martial arts can use their skills to defend themselves.

Different martial arts have different dress codes, but students must always be clean and tidy. All training suits are designed to be strong, comfortable and to allow lots of movement. They will often be tied with a belt.

Most martial arts are practised in a special training centre. Mats will be laid out to provide a soft landing when students are thrown to the ground. Martial arts techniques should *never* be practised outside a class.

Grades and belts

The colour of the belt shows how advanced a student is. Generally the grades are as follows:

Beginner	White
	Yellow
	Orange
	Green
	Blue
	Purple
	Brown
Advanced	Black

A martial artist throws his opponent who uses a 'break fall' to stop himself getting hurt.

Aikido ("i-key-doe"): is a Japanese martial art. By blending various moves, throws and locks, the martial artist uses the energy and motion of the attacker and turns it back on them.

Two Capoeira students practising.

Capoeira ("cap-o-air-ra"): is a martial art that was started in Brazil, by African slaves. It combines dance, music and acrobatics with fighting moves. It is very graceful, flowing and a powerful martial art.

Karate: is a Japanese martial art. In general, it relies on practising repeated moves – punches, kicks, knee and elbow strikes and 'open-hand' techniques.

Kung fu: describes most Chinese martial arts. There are two major types: southern styles use techniques of strength and power, and northern styles use fluid, fast and open movements.

Judo: Judo is a Japanese martial art and combative sport. It involves throwing techniques and grappling on the ground with pins, locks and chokes.

Ninjitsu: combines physical, mental and spiritual skills. It was originally used in the training of spies. There are 18 different levels of training including: spying skills, horsemanship, armed and unarmed combat, disguise, escape and concealment techniques.

Taekwondo ("tie-kwon-doe"): is a Korean martial art that uses 'fist and feet' techniques – kicks, jumps, spins, hand-strikes and blocks.

Glossary

abseil	to go straight down a vertical surface using ropes to stop yourself falling
accelerate	to move more quickly
analytical	to use mental skills that require detailed examination or logic
belaying	a way of controlling rope so that a climber does not fall very far
dehydrated	to lose a large amount of water
deploy	to bring into action
descend	to go down
dilate	to make wider or larger
disorientate	to lose your sense of direction
free fall	to fall quickly
horizontal	flat and level, the opposite of vertical
manoeuvres	a series of physical movements requiring skill and care
predictable	to be able to state that something will happen in the future
serrated	having a jagged edge
shackle	a metal link
stamina	to keep going mentally or physically
urban	about a town or city

Index